Manifesto of a Blossoming Supervillain

By Lincoln Christie

The characters and events in this book are fictitious. Any similarity to real persons, living or dead, is coincidental and not intended by the author.

ISBN: 9798223607762

MANIFESTO OF A BLOSSOMING SUPERVILLAIN

First edition, May 17, 2023

For Gabi
When I say 'burn it down' you pass me the gasoline

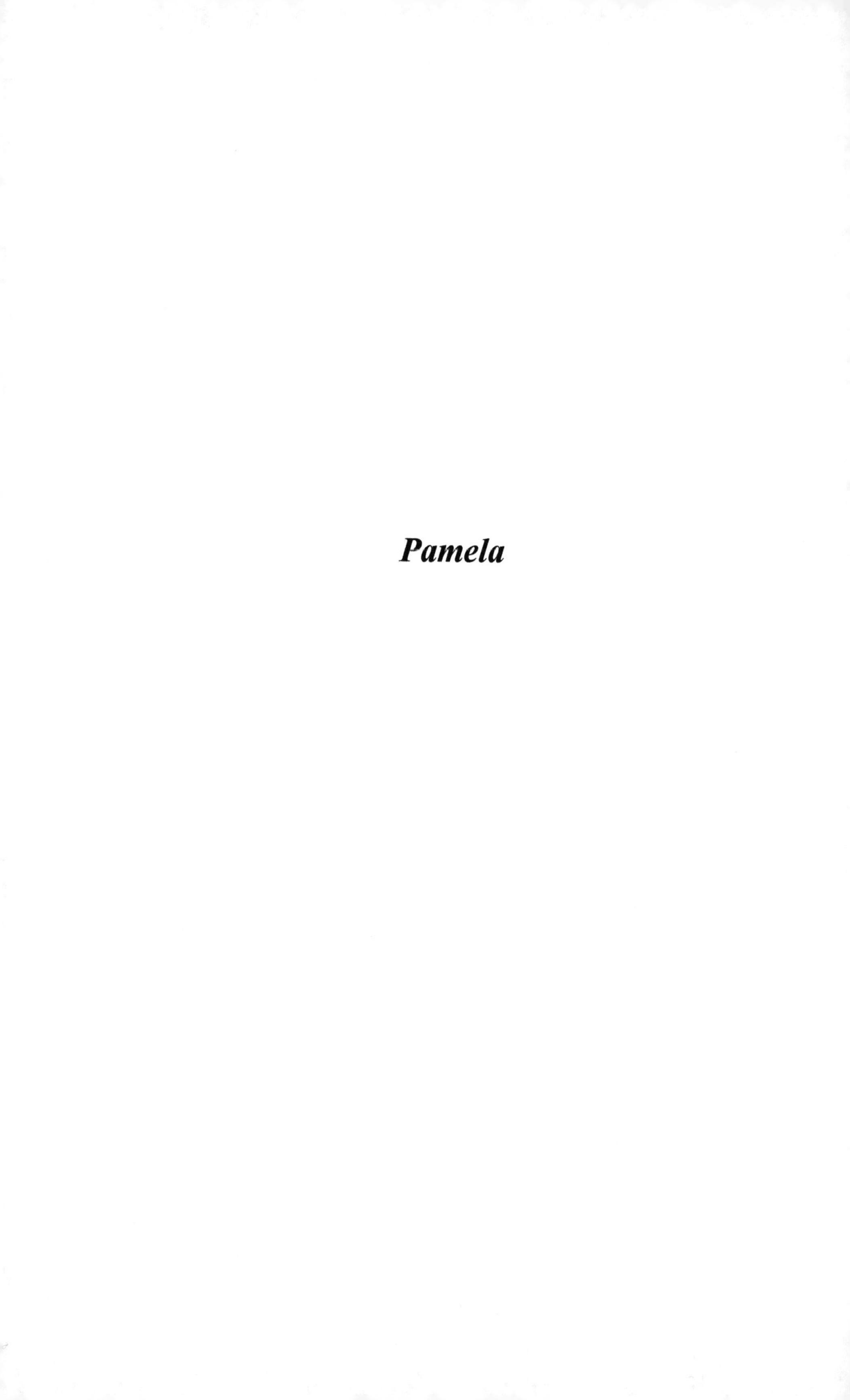

Pamela

Lilith

They say a man made me.
What a funny sort of jest.

As if I was not in the garden every morning
As if my hands were not stained soil brown
As if my PhD was a party trick

I wouldn't lie under Adam, so he made me a witch;
Nature is a woman and nature is green
Any wonder they called me Ivy?

A man made me:
>   Play the sweet rose
>   Grow thorns
>   Grow poison
>   Turn my hands into grasping vines
>   Snap my petals shut tight

But a man did not make: Me.

I would lie beside but not beneath
I laid beside whoever I wanted
I stood beside whoever I wanted
including my fellow doctorates
now I'm a Venus fly trap.

I would scream when they tried to smother me
Weeds strangled me
so I grew deeper roots and ripped them apart
and they called me a monster for it.

It makes me wonder if those they call demons
were merely misunderstood mortals
Medusa and Lilith
Persephone and Ishtar
all started out as maidens and became
the queens of death.
Well then so shall I.
After all
plants grow best in fields of blood.

Ninety Men

My hit list is not long.
Ninety men long
Ninety fat rolls of flesh long
Ninety limp dicks long
Ninety men missing souls who own the
gnawing machine monsters
who kill the world.

Ninety men who own the company
that owns the company
that owns the company
that owns the company
that bleeds us dry.

Ninety men who pay the politicians
and rape the land
and gorge on our wallets.
Ninety men who long for a woman
who are weak for a woman
that lets them think
they are kings instead of tyrants.

Ninety men who made the noose
that strangles the world.
We are eight billion and
the earth is so much more than us.

Taking a drop of water does not diminish the ocean.

My hit list is not long.
It is only ninety men.

Mother and Her Daughters

Once, we carved her out of clay,
the first of gods.
We called the land the cradle,
because it reminded us of her thighs
and how we'd lie in her lap and she'd tell us
stories.

Once we named the storms, the sea,
the ravishing fires after her.
She had brought us into this world—
who else had the right to take us out again?
She gave us life, so who else birthed the plants?
The hands of men are too rough,
they do not make good planters.
They scatter their seeds too wide
and few grow where planted
but Mother's always flower and blossom.

Ships of air and land and water
all bear her name.
What else should we call such powerful things?
Who else is so powerful?
Who else can defy the laws of gods?

Once, we cried out *Mother*
and the earth knew us.
Now we call her *mine*
and the earth still knows us;
why else does she weep?
Did you not know that every hurricane
every giant mountain range of waves
are her tears
and that when the snow bears down with howls
that is because her tears are frozen?

Mother lost her voice. Her daughters
cry and scream and rage
yet none hear them.
None hear us.
once we were called *priestess*

those who knew even better called us *gardeners*.

Mother and her many daughters
plundered like so many machines in the earth
drilling into the earth
digging large clawed steel hands into the earth
laughing 'but it's so soft and wet'
'surely we were meant to plant here,'
Fracking the slick from the earth and shaking hands over it.

Once we worshipped her—
with every bit of earth we tended.
with every dance to the stars.
with every time the moon grew too full and spilled over.
Didn't you know
there is always a reaping?
When autumn comes and the plants must be collected
didn't you know there's a tithe to the gods?

Didn't you know that the job of a gardener
is to pluck out the weeds and the sick ones?

Once we knew her
and called her Mother.
Now she is angry and she will be called
Goddess.

Out of the Wasteland

They say men killed the world.
There is a reason the harbingers of death
were men.
On their red and black and pale horses
it is always men who start the war.

I see it all too clearly
with every tree that falls
my heart cracking with every chunk of ice that breaks free
from the cold twin hearts of the mother.

Men kill the world, they said.
But the men were so inconsiderate
as to die before they could reap what they had sown;
they leave that task to the women:
harvest and find a way to eat it.

The men die and the women live on and must find a way to
Live on.
We cannot go on and yet.

They always treat roses and orchids like women's flowers;
gift them to your lover, if she's a woman.
I always thought of them as men's flowers
men's hearts
so soft and fragile and needing constant care,
the right water the right soil the right sunlight;
Not too much of this,
Not too little of that.

Women are thorn bushes.
We are not pretty enough, not tamable enough,
We must be pruned and cut down and ripped up by our roots.

But we will grow out of the wasteland, oh,
when there is nothing left but the wasteland,
my roots will still be there.
My ivy will still be there, my thornbushes,
clinging and ugly and with roots too strong and too deep
for you to ever destroy.

Out of the wasteland,
We are all that will be left,
when you men are finished pruning each other.

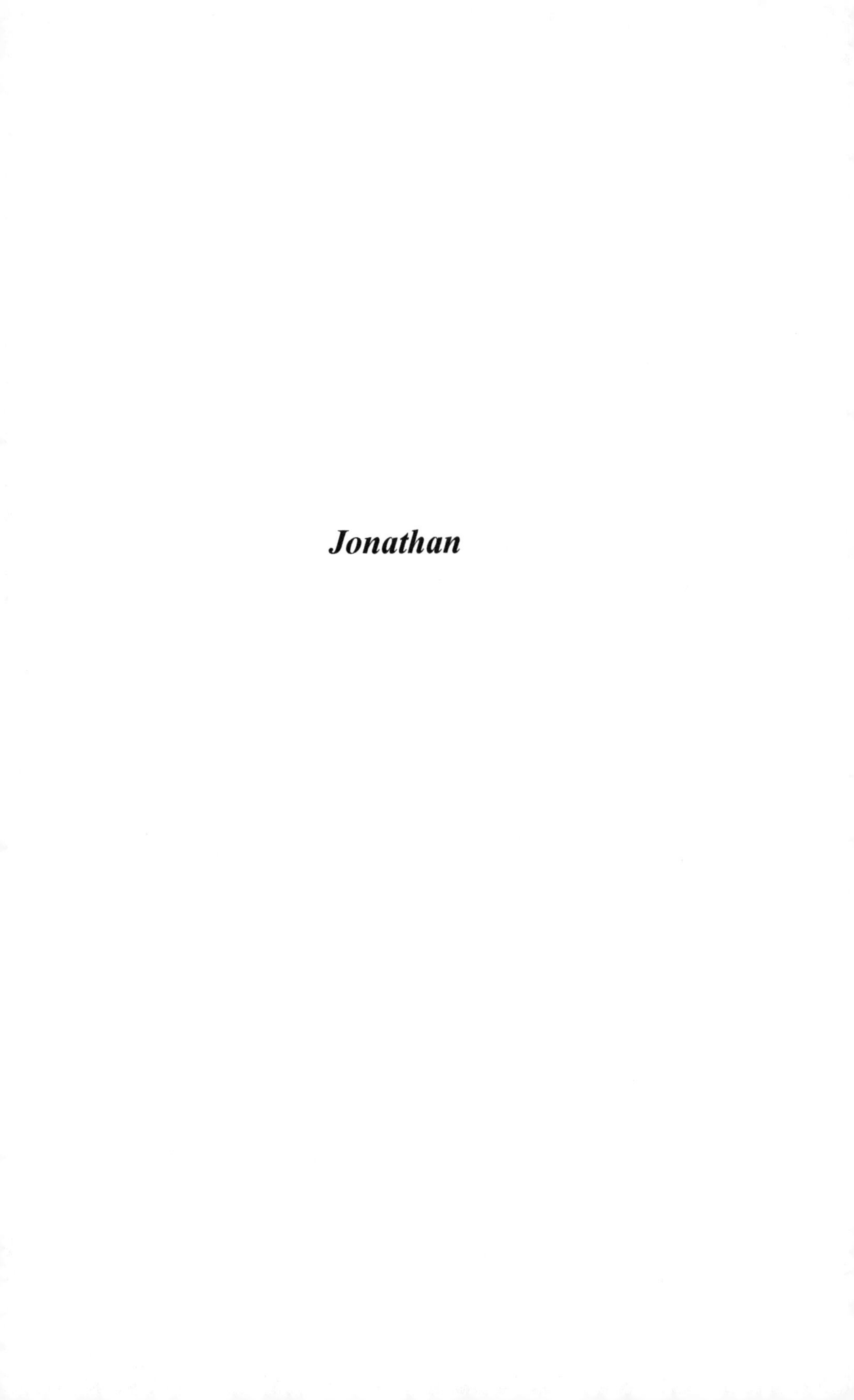

Jonathan

How I Chose My Name

Did you know that the Great Depression didn't end
until the United States involved itself in the second World War?
We waited until the last minute to join, which
doesn't exactly look good on us later,
but then, when does anything we've done look good on us
later?

I suppose some will laugh it off and say it's growing pains.

History shows:
countries are unified when they have a common enemy.
After the attacks on the twin towers on September 11, 2001, the
patriotism—
no
jingoism, I suppose I should say. Nationalism—
it had never been stronger.

Did you know that two comic book writers had to stir up support for
the war?
Many people actually thought that Hitler wasn't so bad
and that the Jews should take care of themselves.
They thought Europe's problems should stay in Europe.
America first.
I'd laugh but it would hurt my throat. Public fervor had to be whipped
up and so a hero was created—
a hero to fight Hitler, a hero that showed the public which side they
were on.
Steve gave them an enemy,
and so they united.

The states were never stronger than when they were fighting the
British.

And so maybe…
Maybe, if I…

My hero cannot exist without a villain, after all, and I know he longs
for that day without villains to come.
But what shall happen when he is no longer around to inspire?

What happens when people don't have a hero to whom they can look
up?
All that remains is a villain.

A man of straw.

He burns so easily, does he not?
Fire makes people feel grand and big,
like they're a part of something.
There's a reason that the military recruits through video games,
through the players with high scores.
You felt good shooting at this enemy, did you not?
The straw burns so easily, does it not?
Do you feel victorious and united, lighting the torches together?

Looking up on the pedestal unites people only so long as the Messiah
has not fallen.
Spoiler alert:
he always falls.
Creation is easier than maintenance,
and destruction is even easier than that.
Give them something to cheer and you have them for a day.

Give them something to fear and you have them for years.

Lucifer Volunteered for the Role

I suppose it's stupid of me to think that people can change.
I'll be honest, when I was younger,
I wanted to outrage people and scare them,
because it made me feel like I had power
and it gave me attention that I controlled for once.
Usually if I had attention it was because I did something wrong.
If I upset people on purpose,
at least then I was holding onto the controls.

I think that's why people cut themselves,
why they leap off buildings.
Sure, it's pain and sure, they're dying,
but at least it was pain that they choose to build for themselves
instead of merely their brains betraying them with
imbalanced chemicals.

Free will, I think, is the greatest love story of humanity.
The Enkindu that Gilgamesh will forever chase,
The Patroclus that Achilles will forever mourn,
The Eurydice that Orpheus cannot help but look back on
and in so, doing lose forever.

So, I made people angry.
I made people scared.
It wasn't just attention and it wasn't just my choosing.
It was the idea of *power*.
Free will might be our Juliet,
but power is our heroin.
There's a reason that Hamlet abandoned Ophelia to kill Claudius.
When people were afraid of me, when they were off their guard, I had
power.
And I think it was the one moment I could get them to
possibly
change their minds about me.

I can be honest and admit that in the end they never really changed in
their hearts.
They never respected me,
they still hated me.
But oh, God, how they *feared* me.

And that fear kept them from punching me out in the schoolyard
anymore.
Mmmmm heroin.

I have great respect for the people who take the time to be kind,
who slowly change the minds of the intolerant and prejudiced.
We need those sorts of people in the world, truly we do.
The slow-working prophets, the Johns who baptize.

I prefer to upturn the tables in the temple.

I'm not here to change minds, you see.
I'm not here to change your *hearts*.
The little blackened coal-piece in your chest is welcome to think
whatever it wants,
of me or of others.
I am here to *scare* you.
You can think or feel whatever you desire.
I'm not here to judge your private thoughts.
I'm not even here to judge what you fuck your fist to in the bedroom.
I'm here to stop you from doing any of it in the streets.
A little shame is healthy. A little fear is pleasant.
After all, we don't want people masturbating at the bus stop.
I don't want you wearing your swastikas at a bar,
I don't want you calling me a faggot in front of the grocery store.
You can hate us in our hearts all you damn well please
but I'm going to make you so *fucking* scared to touch us,
You won't dare show it on the streets.

Other people, better people,
the ones who dunk you slowly and gently under the holy water—
They can change your hearts.
I welcome the way that their soft words and beckoning hands lead you
to the cooling stream.
But coaxing a horse takes time.
And our lives are short.
Our lives are shortened by your fires,
your chants,
your white hoods,
your bullies in blue.
You can coax the ones who remain, I'll make sure they remain afraid.
For every twisted corpse on the news,
I strike fear.

I'm here to make you afraid,
I'm here to make you know you can't get away with your violence,
I'm here so you don't fucking raise a hand or a word because you know
you'll be the next fucking body on the television screens.
You'll be the next corpse with a spider crawling out of its mouth,
the purest thing to ever come out of your mouth,
you'll be the next bloated body in blue.

My hatred is stronger than yours.

I'm not looking for change.
The saints can do that, and they are welcome to their
ascension.
The Devil does just as much good for the church
as Mother Mary.

Why Ectoplasm is Intangible

On Halloween I hear the dead.
I was told that is the night they rise.
The specters of our failures and fathers
the imprints of the lives we might have lived.

I waited as a child to see their twisting writhing wraiths,
the wrathful whispers of the things we were not good enough to
become.
I thought they would be as they show in film and storybooks;
Centuries of human depiction cannot be entirely wrong, or so I thought,
a foolish youth.

On Halloween I hear the dead,
But they do not take the shapes that we all so easily assign them.
Those stories and scriptures are another lie, another comfort;
even as we lie shivering in our beds,
it is so much easier to tell ourselves that the ghosts that haunt us
are the ghosts of people murdered,
not the ghosts of the dreams we strangled with our own cowardice.

I waited as an adult with clearer lenses and sharper instruments,
I wanted to see what true form these apparitions adopted,
and with the belief of childhood replaced
by the conviction of broken boulevards,
my eyes were open the proper way, and I saw.

There were no axe murderers, no damned, no demons:
The lost souls siphoned from the spirit world were no more and no less
than our own.
I realized in that moment that we were all children,
Assigning ourselves the silly fears of our pasts:
giant spiders and scorpions,
the sound of a chopping axe,
the moan of a shuffling corpse,
gnashing, bloodied teeth,
Blood, blood, it all comes down to blood,
to the life we fear we have wasted
and so we conjure up villains who will drain it from us.
The only ghosts that come alive are the only ghosts that exist, the only
ghosts,

The lonely ghosts,
The specters of our losses.
Maybe if we assign spirits to be our tormenters,
our own mistakes become irrelevant.
Your honor, it wasn't me, I wasn't the one who failed myself,
It was the beheaded lady who walked the halls of the castle.
She did it, not me, oh good sir, not me.

I cannot have failed on my own mediocre merit.

On Halloween I hear the dead.
They are not the fallen bodies.
They are the fallen hopes and dreams,
the expectations assigned to us by others.
They step heavily yet lightly through the halls of our hearts,
And with each heartbeat we are convinced that we are not enough,
that we have not earned our lives.
And so we make up monsters to steal the life from us, we make up a
man to blame.
We speak of those who passed with business unfinished,
a bogeyman so that we will not make the same mistakes.
The dead's voices are loud, and I speak for them.
You do not fear the masked maniac,
the chainsaw's cannibal,
the demonic cluster of chorusing ghouls,
You fear you are less than.
I speak your failures to your face and remove the masks.

On Halloween I hear the dead,
and the rest of the year,
you hear me.

I Learned it in THEA 202: Script Analysis

Did you know I took acting classes in college? Yeah. I didn't exactly enjoy it. My advisor told me it might be helpful in understanding people—that acting is psychology, just overshadowed by fiction. I found much of it to be an exercise in trauma.

Stanislavski tells us to recall emotional memories from our past that match the emotion of the character in the moment, and use that for our scene. He talks about how it all must be natural. In the moment, in the moment, it's always in the moment.

Strasberg took it further, as did Adler. Meisner went sideways. Chekov turned it inside-out and he is the only one who made any sense to me.

I wasn't much into the improv. I'm not very funny, or so I've been told. But it's come in handy, made me quicker on my feet, given me better reaction times. It was my improv teacher that said it.

"Motivation is all about love."

I scoffed. I was never one to be quiet about my opinions, especially my disdain. That was when he looked me in the eye and asked me, "Why do people hate?"

I was thrown by the question—I started to explain, gave answers that any of my other professors would have applauded, but he just shook his head.

"People hate because they're afraid," he said. "People don't understand things they don't know, so they're scared. And people hate being scared because it means they're helpless, so it's easier to hate, because hate is active. Hate makes them feel powerful again."

Then it's fear, I thought. Fear is the point from where all people operate. When I said as much, my professor shook his head.

"You're close, but where does fear come from?"

I told him that the proper phrasing would be, "from whence it comes," which I can admit is more about my own inability to admit that I don't know something rather than being about my need to correct people. I'm told I correct people too much, that I'm too pedantic, but I see no reason not to be. People need to know when they're wrong.

People are always ready to tell me when I'm wrong, after all. When I say the wrong thing, when I'm rude, when I'm… cold.

My professor didn't let my comment bother him. Instead, he said, "People are afraid, because they don't want to lose what they love.

Whether it's their life, a loved one, a meal—or less tangible. Their understanding, their viewpoint, their lives as they know it."

Hate comes from fear comes from love.

A love of who one is, a love of comforts, a love of the familiar.

To change one's mind is to go into the unknown.

I thought about what I feared: That someone else would prove themselves a stronger intellect, that the bullies who had so abused me in my youth would take my life. It had felt as if they could when they had loomed over me, even though now as an adult they seem so small.

Children are vicious creatures.

(Adults are cowards but no less psychopathic.)

I realized that all that I had ever feared, both now and in the grip of gasping adolescence,
was that something I loved would be stolen. Whether it was as primitive and encoded as my life, or something more ethereal like my sense of self—my sense of the world—or my conviction that I was the smartest.

I think it makes me the most effective villain, if I can be honest instead of modest (and I'm never modest). The others… they simply wish to cause chaos, to outrage. They're children who want attention from their parents, from the world, and so they lash out. They remain stuck in the notion that any attention is good attention. Otherwise, they have a cause, a crusade, and they will preach their religion to the world whether the world wishes to hear it or not. A few of them are just in it for the money and I respect that.

But if you wish to preach, you first have to get people to listen, and if you want attention, then you'll certainly get it—but will it warm you at the end of the day when you still end up alone? I don't bother with attempts at education. Nor do I wish to nail my qualms to the commissioner's desktop.

I simply wish to expose to people their basic instincts, and make them feel as I felt all of my life. I wish for them to share the pain that I have felt, and in that moment, I am no longer alone.

The way to spread that fear, to make them afraid as I am afraid, is not to simply put them in a pit of snakes
…although, I admit that is a classic. I'm quite proud of that one. Even if it is rather cliché and banal.

Listen. My point is, I scare people the most, I am the most feared, because I do not strike at what people *think* they fear.

I do not strike at their hatred.

I peel the onion back all the way to the bleeding raw tiny little heart of it all, where the smell of norepinephrine is strongest, and I insert my probe, oh so delicately, into what they *love*.

I got an 'A' in the class, by the way.

Fuchsia Emerald Alizarin Rose

Maybe I should dress in rainbows.
They say darkness is what man fears most
his first invention was
fire
to keep the darkness at bay.

But I see the bright colors—
how you flinch away
cast your eyes down like
neon vermillion chartreuse
will be what blinds you.

Man prefers darkness.
He prefers not to see
He cannot handle it
He shrinks back, he obfuscates, he dances
around
the subject
Oh, how you long for monochrome.

The idea of something you hate and fear
living in broad daylight
scares you more than any shifting shadow.
Maybe instead of nighttime terrors
erasing light
I should have warped what light was there;
Scattered your fractal fears like kaleidoscopes.

The pride, you say, the audacity.
The monster in the dark is expected
more welcomed
than the Other soaking up the sun

Instead of enveloping you in my strawman smoke
maybe I should use a stained-glass magnifying lens.
I always loved to watch bugs squirm
angle it just right to burn the ants
Humans are even better—
I can hear your screams.

Tell me true, is it the scarecrow you hate,
or the cornfield?
You burn down both but only blame one.

Maybe if I wore rainbows
smeared my Sodom mouth over your lips
I wouldn't need fear gas
at all.

Selina

Home

They say that cats don't have a home.
I don't know what cats they've met but they're not like any cats I
know.
The trick with cats is to understand that you're not in charge;
they are.
Once they pick a home,
and they've decided it's you,
you can't get rid of them.
It's not allowed.
Cats understand home better than anyone else.

I understand home better than anyone else.

I lost mine.
It was a long time ago, now. I don't remember what it felt like.
I just remember the loss.
It lodged in my chest and it still hasn't left.
As I wandered through Europe I looked like a native—
fooled the Italians, the French, the Swiss.
Too sophisticated for the Brits and too luxurious for the Scandinavians
they thought I was Greek or Russian.
And I loved it all,
I was loved by all,
but God,
it sure wasn't home.

The first person to understand me was a vase in a museum.
The little plastic plaque said it came from the Sudan.
I pressed the pads of my fingers to the ghost of the glass,
and for the first time in years, I
        b r e a t h e d.

Red tape is no match for kitty claws, snip snip
and the paperwork, oh, the paperwork;
if I know a man who can forge a passport, he can forge anything.
office locks are child's toys
Wasn't the vase always there?
Was the vase never there?
Well how else can you explain the switch?
It wasn't Cairo, it wasn't Tehran, it wasn't Delhi,

here, kitty kitty kitty
'twas I who swiped the stuff.

If I picked up some jewels along the way, well,
they're just stones.
Sparkly stones that glisten and glitter and flicker across your eyes,
blind you.
People say I'm stupid to be so showy,
but it was never about the shinies.
Nobody sees the mask used in coming-of-age ceremonies in the Congo,
the knife that scraped against ribs in the Andes
the woman of clay that was worshipped in the Caribbean.
It's diamonds.
Diamonds are a girl's best friend.
The papers are the paperwork,
journalistic integrity is my best friend—
just like Belgium's African honor, it doesn't exist.

They say you try to give others what you never had,
They say you love others the way you want to be loved,
Well, then, I have never loved anyone as much as I love artifacts.
I steal jewels and I rehome lost kittens,
little lost kittens like me.
White wastrels stole them so now I return them,
and the blogs are all about the emerald bracelet
(What do you want me to say? It complimented my eyes.)
Rubies are just as bloody but much more interesting than a South
African chess set.
I found your lost cat, Guatemala,
I microchipped her for you.

And then when I curl up in my little cat bed
knowing others are rehomed makes me sleep;
it's healthier than catnip and makes the blank space on my adoption
papers
feel just a little bit smaller.

I Think You Should Listen to More Cyndi Lauper

Everybody wants to know why I do it.
Has it never occurred to you, World's Greatest Detective,
that someone doesn't need a tragic reason to do what I do?
Did you miss the part where I break into the safes of the rich and safe?
The part where I play with their pretty jewels?
I'm not here to stylize my unhealthy coping mechanisms,
there's no trauma to unpack like a Tiffany's box,
no mental illness to prop up with perpetrations.

I'm here because it's *fun.*

Oh, handsome, do you remember that? Fun?
To do something simply for the rush?
When was the last time somebody got hurt, huh?
Between the insurance payout and the bragging rights,
I'm the best thing that ever happened to these peacocks.

Look, you and I both know that if you ever slapped the cuffs on me—
The proper cuffs, not the fur-lined ones—
I wouldn't be headed to the asylum.
I'm the lunch break,
I'm the Saturday matinee,
I'm the dipping out ten minutes early on Friday.
Haven't you ever wanted to break into a place just to see if you could?
Haven't you ever wanted to wander through a museum when it's dark
and sacred,
all alone except for the shadows on the paintings?
Haven't you ever wanted the thrill up your spine
and in your stomach,
of knowing you did something illegal
wrong
dirty
and got away with it?

I grew up with well-off parents, lost 'em too soon.
Nothing all that dramatic—
illness for my mother—
car crash for my father—
My mother used to dance ballet.
Ballet and yoga, it's how I stay limber.

What? The splits don't do themselves.
There was no injustice to rail against for me,
but God, how I wanted what I'd lost—
the love I'd lost, the fun I'd lost—
so now I steal it for myself.
And it's *fun*.

Listen, when you look back on your life,
I want you to ask yourself:
in between the vertebrae of the lives you saved,
the oceans you cleaned,
the forests you planted,
the stomachs you fed,
the scholarships you funded,
the criminals you stopped—
Did you have fun?
Deep in that rigid lawful good spine of yours,
lurking in the fluid that still holds flexibility,
tell me, "caped crusader"—
hey, handsome, tell me:
did you have fun?

Basil

Gardens of the World with Audrey Hepburn

One time, my therapist asked me why I did it.
Generally, therapists try to avoid that question.
It's a complicated Christmas light snarl of a question.
Even if we answered honestly,
would we even know we were telling the truth?
But she did ask me, a few months in.
I think she wanted to get a read on where my thoughts were.
Perhaps she wanted to get a read on herself, to see if she could tell
when I was lying.
I started to tell her about the murders, and she held up a hand.
She holds up her hand a lot, like a traffic cop.
That's the physical quirk I would use to build up my impression of her,
were I inclined to impersonate her and escape.

She said she wanted to know why I agreed to be

injected

with the cocktail.

Why I chose to return to the garden and become clay.
I replied,

"Have you ever seen a picture of Audrey Hepburn when she's old?"

That stopped her faster than any traffic cop.
I was surprised, but in a pleasant sort of way,
when she pulled out her phone to look up the actress.

"Oh," she said. "I always thought she died young."

Yeah.
That's what most people think.

No one shows you the stars when they've started to burn out.
they are preserved at their brightest glow,
when your eyes burn from being forced to gaze upon them.
Amber that aches.

She died when she was sixty-three, which I think is very young.

I'm only fifty myself,
but it still feels young.
It was her choice to leave the acting world and to focus on more
humanitarian projects.
That's not what concerns me.
What concerns me is everyone I meet thinks she died much younger.
They think she died at thirty-five.

And to them,
to the world,
she did.

I hear what people say about us.
I watch as Bruce Willis and Clint Eastwood continue to make "films,"
the same old "films" they've made before.
Slicing and dicing the bad guys, making their own days and no one
else's.
I can feel the pity that rolls off the audience.
The only people who enjoy those movies are the other old men
who want to believe that their glory days are also not also truly behind
them.

I understand the fear, for I have it too.
When my knees would crack and my back would ache,
I feared the day I couldn't outrun the predators.
It doesn't matter that the predators no longer hunt for our bodies.
I feared them.
But what I feared even more than that was how society hunted the fear
itself.
Society likes us afraid.

If I'm not young and fuckable
what am I?

If she's not young and flawless,
who is she?

I watch her garden documentary and I think,
she's beautiful,
and I realize I've fallen into the trap all over again.
It isn't about beauty at any age;
it's about breathing at any age,
joy at any age,

living at any age.
But a truth only exists so long as others believe in it,
and I knew what we believed.

I let them stick a needle in me.
And hey, they were right. I won't age.
It's all about the fantasy for the audience, anyway.
Most of them don't really want to be me or sleep with me.
They just like to imagine that they do.
A fantasy of a fantasy, Plato's puppet show on the wall and,
even after all these years,
the people still come back to the cave to watch the shadows dance.
They judge the shadows, and call that living.

I will never be Audrey Hepburn, although now I can look like her if I
want to.
But I got it wrong.

I should have just laid down in her garden and become one with the
soil.

Melt

God I'm so fucking tired.
I feel like I was born tired.
My own body weighs a ton.
I can't remember the last time I felt like I drew a full breath.
When was that?

Childhood?

Childhood ended early.
I was around twelve years old that it started.
I don't even know what to call it.
Every time I try to explain it,
I feel like I'm only brushing my fingertips against the void
of what it actually is.
I'm the protagonists of a Lovecraft novel, trying to name the
unnamable.
I was the void.
It wasn't in me or around me,
it was me.

As an adult I can admit I adopted arrogance.
Hubris was my shield and my buckler.
Holding myself together was exhausting, so I relied on others to do it
for me.
If I was charming and talented and loved,
then the rest of the world could hold me together,
and I wouldn't have to rely on myself.

Now the rest of the world thinks I'm dead, or wishes me dead,
and I'm just so fucking tired.
Holding myself together has gone from metaphorical to literal and I
would laugh if I could.
I don't remember how to laugh.
I also don't remember how to cry and that terrifies me even more.
Instead of crying I get headaches.

Prozac doesn't work. None of the medications work.
My body is the softest of clays.
I want to just melt away.

It's not that I actively want to die, I just want to stop feeling so
exhausted.
I want to stop feeling nothing.
I want to stop existing.
Some people might think that sounds peaceful,
or at least better than an active death wish,
but sometimes I think an active death wish would be easier.
I'm so tired but what if—what if I die—
and I'm still the void?
Every day
I force myself to hold together
out of a fear of what will lie beyond,
that it will only be more of the same.
Oh *Christ*, I'm just so fucking tired.

I am the Blank Space

Becoming this way was easy.
I wore a mask long before my face could be molded.
I walked the red carpet,
gave interviews, fan photos,
carefully curated tweets and hashtags;
I cried only when I was alone.

At first it felt like a prison,
the chains of social opinion around my ankles,
but then I returned to the clay like Adam
And I realized:
I had never been safer.

If there was no one around to see me cry and rage
—no one to listen to learn to remember—
who could sling those moments back at me later?
The price of not being myself was that I could be myself;
nobody knew me so nobody hurt me.
There were never former lovers or friends
waiting in the shadows with slick smiles to sell their stories
to the nearest and dearest at the glossy grocery checkout prints.
Or, more accurately,
to post it on social media as a screenshot of a Notes app.
Supermarket tabloids are so blasé now,
but everyone believes a two a.m. confession delivered
via the tracking device in our pockets.

Who I was would never be good enough,
so why be anyone?
Why even let them see me?

The betrayal that I should have seen coming
was written on the wall of my dressing room
two agents and ten years ago.
Now I can never be betrayed.
You can't betray someone you don't know.
I don't even leave a fingerprint
much less a digital one.

I am perfect as they want me to be,

The lover, the man, the woman they want me to be,
I am everyone and no one and at last
I have created the person that everyone loves:
the person who can be anyone, so long as that person is wanted.
I choose my face,
my body,
my voice,
and none of it is me,
and I go home and I collapse into a blob that is neither beautiful nor
ugly but simply exists
and I cry alone.

I cry alone, and I'm safe.

(Re)Mold

They say there've been about ten of us.
Eight, actually.
But nobody's really good at keeping count.
I never tell anyone
they're all me.

Nobody tells you what to do
when your body image crisis lies in wait
to pounce when you're thirty-five.

Nobody tells you what to do
when your gender crisis hits
long after you've finished being a teenager.

I remember it so clearly—*the Moment*.
Jealousy sized me up
seized me in its claws
and I googled the actor who replaced me

y'know, whathisname
in the remake of *Dread Castle;*
I looked him up and trawled through images
like some kind of ship
looking for my deadliest catch.

He looked so good on the red carpet.
The kid really knows his angles, I'll give him that.
I thought,
I could never pull off a suit like that.

And there it was.

I spent hours going through
Huntsman
Ozwald Boateng
Tom Ford

God I was really a monster then
the most monstrous I've ever been
and it was to myself.

The thing about *Dread Castle* is
I recall someone at the time—
was it fucking Ebert?—
saying I reminded him of Lugosi
nothing physically imposing
it was all in my eyes.

At the time I took it as a compliment.
Actually, okay, I still do.

But this guy
the kid
He's a—
ladies' man
man's man
man about town

good in a suit
or playing a lumberjack
(for a cover shoot of course)

I'm what the early 00s would call
'metrosexual'

Pause for jazz hands.

So I watched that one show he was in
um
The bad one about ghosts?
It's like the redneck X-Files
and I couldn't stop *staring* at him.

I thought—*you're me I'm you you're me*
the slight bow-legged swagger
the smirking mouth,
the pouting mouth
the broad shoulders
when I wear a leather jacket
I look like I stole my dad's;
he looks born into it.
He manages to be pretty while still being a
Man

all I ever managed was
well you know what they say about skinny waifs
like me.

Might as well strap on a pair of wings.

I realized—*he's not me I'm not him*
He was what I
craved
yearned
all those years without knowing I *cravedyearned*

Long story short is the second one of 'us'
looks a lot like him
wouldn't you say?
Blonder, eyes blue instead of green
my smile is different
But,

hello Matt Hagen, at your service.
Real pleased to meet ya, ma'am.

I ain't gonna lie, I loved bein' Matt.
Girls swoon over me
First time in my life
and y'know I ain't never had a problem
lookin' at the men either
but people don't make jokes about it
it's a *relief* for people to assume I like women
an' I do, I sure do

No doubt in yer mind I'm cornfed
An' it's a mighty shame nobody cared to ask 'bout Basil
but I suppose it's just as well;
mighty big lesson in people seein' what they want to see.
Everyone assumed I was a new person
and by God, I felt so much like *me*

The tall person inside a' me, the *tough* person inside a' me
was finally what everyone else saw
and my rage was no longer a source of amusement.
When I say you'd better duck, partner, people *duck*
they eye my fist like it's a viper

and all the coke in Hollywood could never
replace the rush of those moments.

Flirting was finally fun.

But y'know some people thought me too rough,
not that I was,
they *thought* I was.
The backhand backlash when I did somethin' too
well
I say feminine but they used real worse words
I'll give ya two hints
one of 'em was a type of flower
one of 'em was something they used
to burn witches

So I became a witch.

Sondra Fuller, it's a pleasure, thank you.
Oh, this old thing?
I got it when I was in Paris for Fashion Week
well yes, but it's simply madness, darling,
I think running with the bulls leads to less trampling.

You have no idea what a relief it was to be delicate
and *like* it.
I stared at my hands for hours after I got the shape just right.
They were such darling little things!
Fine tapered fingers
my movements balletic
You could pick me up with one arm easy as anything.

I was quite old-fashioned, skirts every day,
dresses that fit and that flared
cheeky little pump heels
corsets that hugged me tight and made me feel more solid
like I was flesh and bone again

Oh, I was enraptured with the sight of my breasts
peeking out from a well-fitted strapless top
and my voice!
Finally I could sing along with the sopranos.
My neighbors plotted my death

over how many times I sang at the
top of my clay-filled lungs

the way something inside me settled
when I could nestle under a lover's arm
because at last I was short enough for it

I could be *soft*
and not simply because of the clay
I was handled gently
with care
and it was no longer assumed
I could do everything on my own
supportless weightless

but then the catcalls
the condescension
the callousness
the casual comments

I was told I should be a phone sex line operator with that voice
I was told I was a tease if I changed my mind and stopped flirting
I was told I was too arrogant

stuck up
cold
harsh.

Bitch.

People—even friends—
mentioned my rage like it was a puppy
calling its name with a coo in their voice
"a tiny girl full of rage"
they would laugh

Oh, darling, I promise you,
my fists were still vipers.

I missed my body being big enough to hold my rage
I missed being able to look people in the eye without heels
I missed having sex with other men as a man

So then I was
Cassius
Cassius "Clay" Payne
Geddit?
Eh, so few people geddit.
Ah well
just a little joke between me, myself, and I then
and there are so many mes and myselves and Is

I've molded and remolded myself until
I don't know anymore what name fits
I don't know what body fits

Woman or man? Tall or short?
Spun glass Sondra or metal forged Matt?
Or perhaps it's the other way around.
I pour more and more clay into the craving cavern

heismesheismeIamme

I am none

I'm the fluid in gender
always want what I can't have
but like the way I am;
the potter's wheel is never still
I mold and mold and
mold and mold and mold
and moldandmoldand

Harley

Extreme Personalities

I wasn't really popular at the asylum.
Before I was a patient here, I mean.
There was talk later on that a first-year employee fresh out of her residency
should never have been given such a dangerous inmate to profile.
I think there was hope that if I had to handle him
I'd give up and quit.

The hair dryer incident was how it all started.
We had a patient who said she was always scared when she left home
that she had forgotten to unplug her hair dryer.
I told her to just take the hair dryer with her.
They didn't like that.

The next one was the stove.
"I'm always going home because I'm scared I left it on."
I told my patient to set up a camera with a live feed.
Pet parents do it all the time.
That way he could always just check the camera and see that the stove was off
and everything was okay.

When I told a patient to try talking politely to his voices,
to see if they could all become friends,
I was told to change his medication and that I was being reassigned.

The quote from my job interview has been played so much I hate the sound of my own voice.
I've always been attracted to...
As if I have some kind of fetish.
As if our only job is to make people conform to the reality we've assigned as valid.
My job isn't to tell you what's real.
My job is to help you be happy.

I Didn't Earn $120k in Student Debt for This

When most people hear the word doctor they think "PhD."
A doctorate.
It's actually M.D.
I got my medical degree—
which is impossible to obtain through sex,
by the way.

I start all of my sessions like this nowadays, now that I'm on the other
couch.
Most people get this shocked look in their eyes
like they didn't expect me to rip away the curtain and play Toto
exposing the emerald emperor beneath.

The color green means envy, y'know.

I didn't sleep with my professors.
I did sleep with a T.A., once.
It wasn't because he would get my grades up, I was already pulling As.
He was just really hot
and I have a history of falling for the wrong
men.
I don't know if you noticed that.
Mostly I was too busy banging my fellow students.

Did you know I did a residency and everything?

Yeah, with this one guy—
rich kid, but didn't act like it.
He could hold his liquor like anything.
I see him nowadays on the news sometimes with some model or
another and he's all slurring. Yeah, right.
That guy once did the scorpion trick and he was already ten shots in.
Drunk off one scotch my ass.

I have a great ass, by the way. Not that anybody cares.

But I did my residency.
I was in the hospital for a year,
then my buddy dropped out and I transferred to the asylum.

My point is you can't exactly fudge a diagnosis on a patient in a
hospital.
And you can't exactly fake it when you're performing anatomy for a
final.
Cadavers stink.
I always made Jack keep formaldehyde on hand.
One of our last arguments was about that.
He thought the smell of rotting flesh was better than the smell of
chemicals.
Looking back I can see why he thought that,
why it triggered him.
At the time all I cared about was airborne diseases
and the fact that he tried to strangle me to win the argument.

You know the thing I said about my ass?
I lied.
People care about my ass.
They care about
my breasts
and my waist
and my smile.
They say that's how I got it.
One guy called me "Miss" instead of "Doctor" and I almost punched
him.
The only reason I didn't is because
if I show any signs of violence, Jack gets all the credit.
Which, you know, fuck him.
I knew how to punch long before he got to me.

It's easy to use sex. Society rolled out the red carpet for me and who
was I not to walk it?
But I didn't sleep my way to my medical degree, okay?
Just ask Bruce.

Why I Didn't Dodge the Punch Faster

I didn't know how to say it.
I still don't know how to say it.
I
I dance around it.
What did I expect?

Did you know I used to take dance lessons as a child?
Ballet.
It hurt my legs.
You know they never talk about how ballet
makes you work muscles that've never been worked before.
Hurts like a bitch.
I would cry—my mother would say,
of course it's hard,
What did I expect?

…I'm sorry.
I'm—
talking around it again.
I say—
I say

what happened.
What happened to me.
After it happened.

I don't say
I don't say
I don't say.

The few times I have said it, I've gotten—
Well, if I spare the details, I get pity.
It's generalized pity, though, and I'm not—
I'm not sure how to explain—
I don't want an aspirin.
I want Midol.
I want a splint around the broken bone.
So I tell them, specifically.
And they say—
What did you expect?

What did I expect?

I don't know what I expected.
I'm not even sure that I had expectations.
I just.
Felt.
He was the one with expectations.
Plans.
That's something I have to get used to.
He planned all this, from the beginning,

You're a tenacious one
You're a smart one
Didn't know that shrinks could be beautiful.

Those lines were lies—
What did I expect?

He expected
he'd kill me or leave me behind.
You hang on like a fungus, ah,
But what else did I expect?

His words. Not mine.
I can't always recall;
were those mine or his?
It's called 'gaslighting', dear
I know, I studied it in school.
What did you expect?

If I was really smart—
some say, and
I say, to my mirror I say—

If I was really smart.

I've been told it happens to smart people, too.
Sometimes the smartest people are the easiest to suck in.
They think they're too smart to ever be fooled.
They knew what they expected.

It wasn't that I thought I could outsmart him.

It was more that I wanted to…

Prove myself.
Maybe that's what I expect.

I wanted to prove how good I was,
I wanted so badly to be special
and he used that
Used that
Used me.
Like everyone else—
What did I expect?

We talk a lot about motivations in school.
About why someone did what they did,
how the how is only the first layer,
and beneath it is the truth.
I think really it's that we all want to be loved.
I wanted to be loved.

My coworkers would love me.
My sister would love me.
That's what I expected.

I told her.
She was the first person I told.
She was sad, I'll give her credit for that.
And she said,
But honey, what did you expect?

I think that's just a nice way of saying,
It's your fault.
Nobody would ever say it's my fault,
at least not to my face.
I can watch the news and read the articles, y'know.
I'm not cut off from the outside world,
here.
The talk show segment was especially…
entertaining.

But to my face, they never say it's my fault.
They just act like I should have known better.
I wasn't asking for it.

I didn't put a sign on the front door that said
BURGLARS ENTER HERE
But I left the door unlocked.
What did I expect.

The only people who get it are the people who saw it,
who were there.
I love my sister,
but we can't talk.
I've found love is less important than
understanding.
What else can I expect?

Do you know how many times he tried to kill me?

I lost track after seventeen
I stopped being able to tell
which were premeditated,
which were heat of the moment,
which were the times he was dissociating
and didn't even realize what he was doing.
Are there levels of murderous intent?

I don't know what my intent was.
Okay, maybe I do.

Maybe I know my expectations.

I'm not asking for love anymore.
But I'd like some understanding.
Of course nobody has any.
What else did I expect?

The Letter I Carved on My Cell Wall (Before They Took Away My Knife)

he told me I was beautiful
he told me I was smart
he told me he would walk me home
because I'm scared of the dark

he told me I was funny
he told me he loved my laugh
he told me I brought to his life
the sunshine that it lacked

he told me that my voice was sweet
he told me out of all he'd meet
with judging pen click-clacking stares
I was the one who had him beat

he told me my eyes mesmerize
he told me I myself was wise
he told me others envied me
he told me all his alibis

he told me he loved the color green
and that my ass was the best he'd seen
that he preferred cocktails to scarlet wine
that a circus was where his dad left him behind

he told me he was so alone
he told me I was on my own
and what together we could make
if my courage I could hone

he told me I was someone who
the void looked back at; that I also knew
about the want to not exist
and what that state of mind could do

he told me no one else could see
the potential that lay inside of me
that nobody else in the world would know
the secret to setting me free

he told me I needed to do as he said
he told me without him I would be dead
he told me all he had given me
and how I'd never get him out of my head

he told me that he loved me true
he told me no one else could too
and nobody had loved me before
so I didn't know he was lying.

Edward

Hercule Poirot and Sherlock Holmes

Walk into a bar in my brain.
They're my oldest companions.
I used to talk to them when I was alone growing up,
which was most of the time
not enough of the time.

It's calming to watch them argue with one another.
They're both far too cerebral in their own ways.
Both have a weakness for women in trouble
but neither of them want to fuck
just like me.
It's nice.

Maybe I should've been a famous amateur detective;
if only I'd been born two centuries ago.
Nowadays,
When you're more interested in solving riddles,
than having sex,
people want to prescribe you something.
Don't you think it's interesting that our greatest detectives are celibate?

That wasn't why I wanted them to be my friends.
I was too young to understand that was why I needed them.
I just needed companionship and there they were,
sitting in my living room ready to commiserate.

They both would be ashamed of me
so I talk to them less now.
Did I turn into Moriarty to better engage Sherlock?
To hold his attention?
My father never gave me attention.
I hate analyzing myself, yet I keep doing it,
my own version of cigarettes.
Who else was I supposed to talk to when my heart raced
and I was scared and alone and
I wanted to end it so many times.
I always imagined they would be the ones to come for me
They would each take a hand and lead me away
and I would become another piece
in the puzzle of the universe,

one of the mathematical equations that sing in the stars.
I thought it would be lovely.

I never ended up pulling that trigger.
One of them would talk me down.
Nobody else talks about their imaginary friends the way I do.
Is everyone simply in denial or am I the only one who's awake?
Or was I the only one who used them as suicide prevention?
I don't always write riddles for the people who exist,
I write them for the men who lived in the books in my head.
I can't quite explain how thinking about an afterlife
where I simply sat with them in a pub
Made me want to live.
If I could explain that, maybe I could explain everything else.
Could they solve me? Would they want to solve me?
There is a compassion and a cold-heartedness that wars inside them
both.
Somehow I learned one and not the other.

Which would they use on me? I find I don't mind
whichever it will be.
I just wish they could get to the bottom of me
and reduce me to a simple whodunnit,
The patient unraveling of all of my strings until we find the original
knot
But maybe if they did they would go away, and I would be alone.
Schrödinger's mystery.

Hercule Poirot and Sherlock Holmes
sit at the base of my skull and whisper to one another:
was it his little gray cells or the angle of his gait
that made him commit murder?

You Asked about My Wallpaper

Mensa tried to claim I was a member.
One of the first articles about me said I went to Harvard.
Yeah, right. I hate New England.

I didn't get it.

You *want* the guy who murdered a city councilman to be your
alumnus?
Look, I'm not exactly hurting in the brains department but
that math is shitty.
Maybe that's why MIT didn't want a piece of me.

If you look over here, you'll see several Ivy League propositions.
Prostitutes don't get as many weekly offers as I did.
I never actually went to college.
Expenses, mostly.
Scholarships aren't available to kids who don't do extracurriculars;
who can't play sports because they're allergic to coordination
and getting noogies in locker rooms
who don't volunteer
whose parents disappeared under mysterious circumstances.

Honestly, I think it all would've been a waste of time.
College is only fifty percent learning;
the rest is socializing.
Yeah when people talk about me and social they put an 'anti' in front
of the latter.
You know, at first I thought it was all the crimes that scared 'em.
Now I think it's my childhood ZIP code.

What do you do with a man who fools everyone and only has a high
school diploma?
What do you do with the kid from the slums who has the police pissing
themselves?
I don't use bombs or guns, except in the occasional booby trap.
No gang affiliations.
I never even had a fake I.D. for underage drinking.
Poor kids aren't allowed to be nerds, right?
The ghettos don't give birth to geniuses.
And yet here I stand.

They wish I went to Harvard.
They wish I was one of them—or one of Them.
But the Other has rules just like they do.
I'm not the monster they know.
If only I was one of them, right?
Anyway, don't add these honorary degrees to my Wikipedia page.
It's just going to make me sound like a total attention whore.
Thanks.

Runaway Wheel

I don't do social media.
The others tried to get me to join a group chat;
I broke out in a cold sweat.
I have to stay on top of the texts,
on top of the texts,
on top of the texts,
on top of the texts,
I have to stay on top of them.

Just like I have to wipe up the kitchen,
wipe it up
clean it up,
wash the dishes
right away,
I can't leave them in the sink
They need to be cleaned up
now now now

God I wanna stop.
I don't even believe in God.
I just want to stop, stop it, *stop it,*
I can't fucking *stop.*
I feel tired all the time but my brain won't stop running
Somebody gave that little hamster a dollop of cocaine.
He's been running that wheel into the ground ever since.

You think I wouldn't stop if I wanted to?
My therapists all say
  let's talk about your father
Oh my fucking god it's not about my father
My brain is just
My *brain* is just
If only I could clean it with a
toothbrush
the way I can clean my bathroom.
You can eat off the floors in there.
Please don't, though.
I'll have to clean it again.

That's the thing—everyone thinks, "oh he's a neat freak."

Gotta clean everything.
Gotta *clean* everything.
Gotta clean *everything*.

Well of course I've gotta clean everything, you keep making it dirty!

But I also gotta
I *also* gotta
I gotta stay on top of the tweets
and the likes
and the posts.
I can't miss any of them,
what if I miss one of them?
I can't ignore a text
or a call
or an email
I have to make the little notification
the *notification*
that ugly
red
notification
It has to go away,
and what if it's important?

The books have to be in the right order
it needs to be the right order
it all has to go a certain way
It has to go *that way*.

Stop calling me an egomaniac.
I mean, yeah I'm an egomaniac.
But hey if you had an IQ at my level,
You'd be one too.
But it's *not* about that
It's not *about* that
It's not about *that*
I am smarter, okay!

But I'm *not*.

If I'm so smart, I could beat my own brain

One time I got arrested in the middle of writing a riddle and

I cried.
Do you have any idea how
embarrassing it is
to have a bunch of grown people with guns
staring at you
as you cry because you can't finish writing
your stupid little poem?

Look up the word 'pathetic' in the dictionary
That incident will be cited.

I haven't been at war with The Bat in years;
I'm at war with myself and I'm fucking losing
Why do you think I'm in here?

He knows I'm losing.

It's not about anyone,
I don't even know what I'd do with the loot
if I actually got away with it.
I just want to prove that I can get away with it,
Get away with it
Get away with it
Prove that I can
subdue myself and stop leaving
fucking riddles.
I can't stop I can't stop
I can't fucking stop
He reads the riddle that I deliver,
he solves the riddle,
he comes to stop me,
It has to go that way my way a certain *way*

Sometimes I think I want him to stop me
Why doesn't he fucking stop me?
Somebody stop this running wheel
this unending wheel
squeak squeak wheel

Please.

stop the hamster.

Riddle Me This

A new intellectual exercise today,
the sort you might find in your school books:

Riddle me this—
If you receive ten apples every week
and only ever eat two
why do you hoard the other eight?

Riddle me this—
if every day you strike him
because you hate the look in his eyes
why not try something new?

Riddle me this—
if every day you throw men in jail
and they walk free only to be thrown in
again
why not provide different consequences?

Riddle me this—
if putting us in asylums does not work
and the looney bin keeps leaking lunacy
why do you keep cramming us inside?

Riddle me this—
if you sit in your ivory penthouses
your blinding statehouses
whitewashed to cover the blood
how can you blame us for tearing you down?

Riddle me this—
if the Mr. Smiths will not take their apples
and give them to us
why should we not take them?

If the police will not arrest he who strikes us
why should we not kill him?

if the rule-strikers will not let us free
if the money-makers will not make *us* money

if you will not share with us
if you will not protect us
if you will simply shove us into the
box

Bruce

Riddle me this:
why should we spare you?

You Never Forget Your First

I've wanted to kill a lot of men—
not that I've succeeded, mind,
or even that I've attempted
(although I have, mind,
many attempts)
but I have yearned for their deaths
as an Austen hero yearns
with curling fingers and propriety's straightjacket;
with an upright spine and
a frantic
mind.

But of all the men I've wanted to kill
(and some women too, mind—
I am equal-opportunity,
it's merely that men
give me so many more reasons
to be tempted by malice)
the first one was my father.

Had it been a war of fists, mind,
he would have felled me
but there are kitchens
filled with knives
there are pharmacies
filled with pills

But, mind,
he had to know that I won.
The dictating despot
had to have had the realization
the flare of fire before the lights
went out.

I parsed the puzzle pieces out
I laid them like stepping stones
and he followed the breadcrumbs
a Hansel with no sainted sister

I will give him this, mind,

he was clever
(as he had always claimed)
but that was never my quibble
no
he was never as clever
as I am.

The first man I wanted to kill was my father.
He was good enough to solve the riddles
and he won the prize:
a free trip to the morgue.

Harvey

Blindsense

When I was a child I heard the term
"colorblind."
I thought it was the way things should be.
Colorblind casting, yeah.
I loved that more than anything.

Colorblind.

When I first saw Justice, scales in her hand,
blindfold making her even more beautiful,
I knew that was where I belonged.

Justice for everyone, justice for anyone,
Good for the good and bad for the bad;
an arm so long it stretched around the world and into the hearts of men.

Justice.

And then I got to law school.
The corruption that led there,
the corruption that bled there,
the bedrock of bad ideas that broke any scaffolding good hearts tried to
build.

The only way to change the system was to be a part of it,
but being a part of it only made me complicit.
The true blindness was revealed:
the blindness of those in need.

Blindness does not mean deafness,
and justice can still hear the jingle of gold coins,
the smooth slip of dollar bills against one another in the hand.
At least prostitutes are honest about their profession.
They take your money right there on the street corner,
they don't wait for back rooms.

Blind.

God, I was blind.
How can I fix anything without power?

How can I gain power without playing the game?
Inside
outside
there is no side.
No side to be on.

Justice is just there.
Prosecutors puncture holes in anything I try to build.
There is nowhere safe without maleness,
without whiteness,
without money,
without complicity in your own subjugation—

But still I tried.
I did everything right.
Everything.
Anything.
I was the whitest knight they'd ever had—
and yes, being a White knight helped,
but I was ready,
I wouldn't dispense a natural tool.
I would hone it like everything else.
I would humble it like everyone else.

And *then*

Vengeance.

It won where justice did not,
it left a deeper mark than the matron
who holds her scales just like a banker
She accounts for every penny and will not give if you don't give,
and I let myself fall in love with the whore.

Vengeance got to me when justice got to no one;
I will not pay the prostitute anymore.
I will not play the pimp anymore.
Vengeance will not fail me.
My face is duplicitous, but at last my heart is honest,
and dark knights are all people remember anyway.

Unlike my lawyer days, my services are free.
That's the difference between a slut and a whore—

we cannot be blind, we must rip off the folds.
The world is in living color and we are trying to make it black and
white.
I will deliver sight to you—
Red is a color too, after all.

The Mirror Test

As babies we are held by our mothers,
shown up to the mirrors,
and asked, *who is the baby in there?*
We look and we stare and we realize we are me
and we never feel as close to our mothers again.

As teenagers we are taught to hold lights up to mirrors,
as our science teachers tell us to watch the lights bounce;
our mirrors are mere reflections, but the light bounces off everything.
The light stays real,
and your reality never feels secure again.

As women, they are warned about the finger test in mirrors;
they hold up the tips of their digits to see if there is a gap,
a distance of a mere inch between yourself and your double,
a distance that measures between honest men and predators
and they never feel safe in restrooms again.

When I looked in the mirror Before,
I knew myself,
and I said I was the original.
Now my finger to glass, I don't see a gap
and I can never be myself again.

Calling Collect

Take your foot off the brake
Hit the accelerator
Shoot them kill them punch them

I'm fine.
Just because my voices now have a face doesn't mean I'm not

fine.

Fine as hell. Fuck her.

I can handle it.
I've always been able to handle it.

Cut yourself hang yourself fling yourself out the window
do it do it do it do it

I'm the sucker with the stolen identity;
He charges the cards and I pick up the tab.
I'm the designated driver who always pays for the drinks

Run away
change your name
stab yourself
eat the second slice of cake

It's not always something dramatic, you know.
I don't know if the

rip the tablecloth

small things are lesser or more dangerous
than the

shoot him

big things.

The road to Hell, I know it well.

Many of my enemies walked down
it until it led to the wooden box in court.

Wooden box in the ground.

Ground is soft lie down
Face down
Don't get back up.

The voice speaks as me now,

speaks out the side of my mouth,

the left side
The Devil's side.
It can speak all it wants, doesn't mean I'll

listen

listen listen listen

to me

To me
it is noise.
Doesn't matter if I ignore it,
if I give in, it's all the same,
it never stops.
A phone that's always ringing.
Picking up only means encouragement to call again,
don't

engage

with the stalker.
I can't shut it up

shut up shut up shut up

but I don't have to

answer

He charges me for all his calls
I pick up the pieces of the things he's smashed

He is me I am him you are me I am you

Big or small, there's always interest on the payments

I'm fine.

I've found a way to handle it
Just because he speaks doesn't mean I have to listen.
He'll speak either way.
Why feed the wyrm if it's never satisfied?

**Consuming and consumed
Ouroboros**

he will never be full
I will never be full.

I'm fine.
It's just that sometimes
I actually answer the phone.

Do it.

We're fine.

Prosecute to Defend

They say I left justice behind
when I started building my guillotine.
Personally, I thought it was rather polite of me to bow to elegant machinery
instead of relying on the strength of fallible men.
Electric chairs don't always work the first time;
lethal injections cause seizures,
twitching in agony until death.
You act as though cutting off a man's head is barbaric
but look at what you do on Death Row.

As a lawyer I defended the people,
argued for innocence until proof of guilt,
fought for those who could not fight for themselves,
stood up to cops and politicians-for-pay,
went *pro bono* more often than not
and every time I saved a life, I knew it was deserved.
But what about the ones who got away every day
with crimes far bigger than the ones with which my defendants were charged?

Police smashed the protestors' faces
and cuffed their hands behind their backs.
Their eyes poured poisoned rain from the pepper spray,
their faces smeared with their own blood.
Politicians passed some measures and blocked others,
concerned only with their own power;
with give and take and tit for tat,
nothing for free,
as constituents starved by gerrymandering.
Corporations lined their pockets, but only in the idea of the idea of money,
so robbing them at gunpoint wouldn't work.
They paid the pipers who used their congressional seats to lead the children away,
what else are we supposed to do?

You make compromises, you make friends,
you tell yourself that when you're the one in power
you can change it all—

but then you're in power
and nothing's changed at all.

Do not some men deserve to die?

Why is it alright when you've done enough
magic tricks in front of the jury
to get them to convict
but when I speak plainly and release the blade
somehow I'm the one who's lost my mind?

I could never convict the true criminals;
no court will ever stop lying for long enough
could never stop letting their palms grow slick with grease.
Call it vengeance, call it insanity,
the method isn't mad if it works.
When they go to prison, they go to a hotel;
they play tennis
have Wifi
extra thick mattresses on their beds.
When they're brought to me, they get nothing but fear.
The river is their mattress
I hope it's thick enough for them.

You look down your noses and call me a monster,
say that I have abandoned my cause—
the oathbreaking knight
But none of those men can hurt you anymore;
no chance for appeal,
no chance for bribes,
Hammurabi's results cannot be disputed.
Look their victims in the eye and say
that these men did not deserve to die.

Unoriginal Sins

My wife—
My ex wife,
She used to say that people were inherently good.
I used to believe that—
To try to believe that.

But if we're inherently good, why was it so easy to be bad?
Why was it so much easier for me to listen to the other half—
Why was it so easy for him to emerge?
I was stressed, I was upset—
People have endured what I endured,
People have endured worse—
Poisonous personalities don't emerge from them like a fungal growth;
Why did it happen?
Why is it so easy to be bad?
How did I break? Was it denial?
Did I deny the bad part of myself for so long it had no choice but to
explode?
No little spurts to let of steam, just the full Mt. St. Helens
Why does it feel like I was fighting my true self?
Is this my true self?

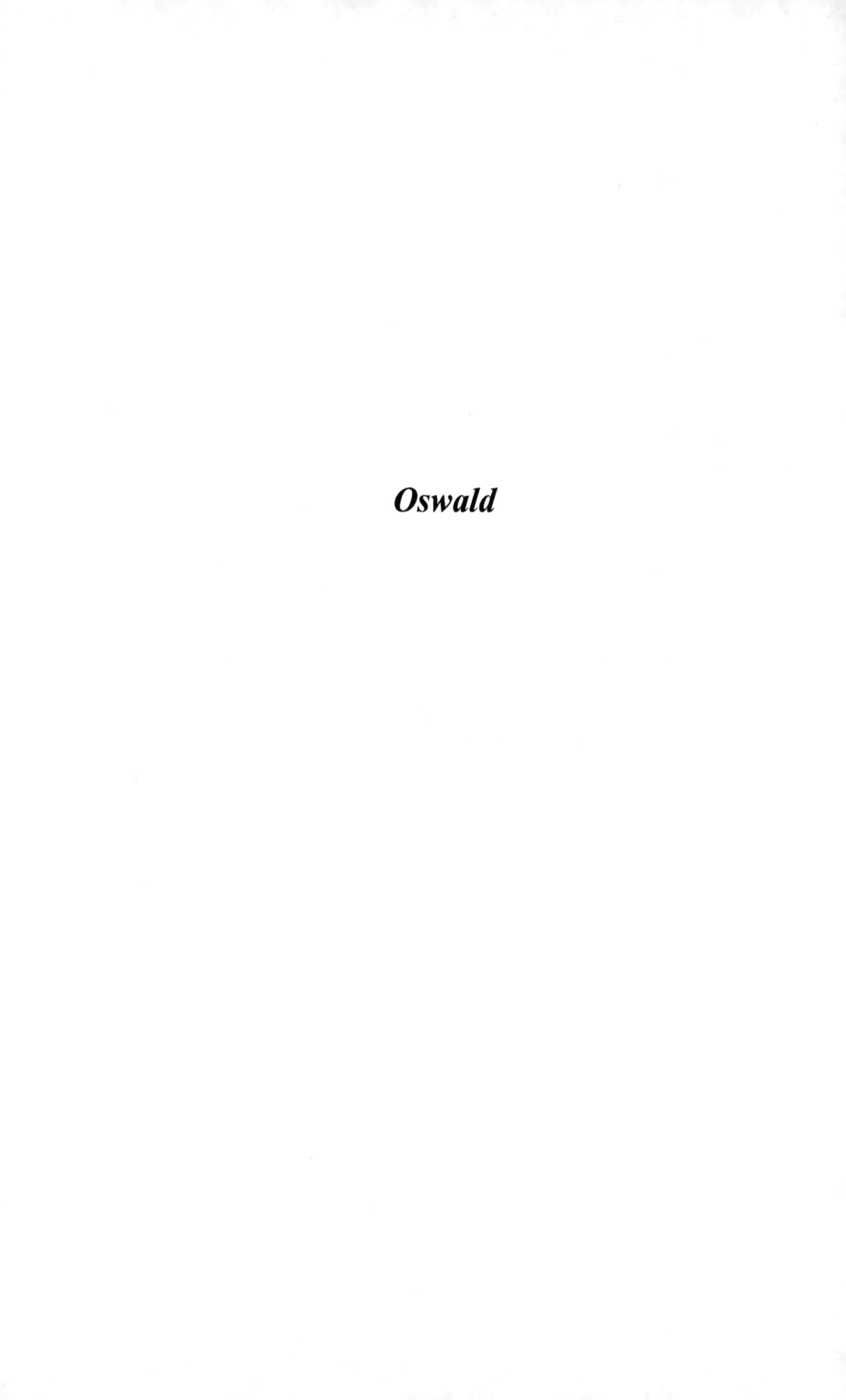

Oswald

Benjamin Franklin is the Best Lover I Ever Had

I'm ugly.
Every time I say that, people wince.
Kind people try to tell me that's not true.
I know,
ahahaha,
I know they think they're helping me by saying that,
but all they're doing is reminding me
that to be ugly is to have lesser value.

I'm fat.
People try to say *plump* or *curvy* or *hefty*;
Any word but *fat*.
Once I was told to say that I was *overweight*.
Overweight means that I am over the weight that is healthy for me
but I'm not.
I am fat.
I might as well be calling myself a slur.

People tiptoe around those words like good Christians
who fish around before saying
lifestyle choices.
I know why.
Somewhere along the way,
people decided that how you looked on the outside was a judge of
character.
I've heard it from the shrinks;
attraction is a twist on the biological desire to find a good mate.
You note a mate's features to see if they're right for you.
We don't value the ability to kill a mammoth anymore
ahahahaha.

We look for
patience,
love,
humor,
morality—
so long as that morality aligns with one's own—
and we believe a person's character is reflected in their looks.
Ergo, ugly people like me are not… good.
We're not… *good.*

I don't know how to describe the exact feeling of knowing you're less than
when there are no other strong markers.
You're not profiled against because you're a person of color.
It's not that you're queer or not cis.
It's something so subtle that I don't think most people even realize it.
It's not second class. It's a half-step above.
It's not first class. It's a half-step below.
Ugly. Fat.
Ahahaha
and what's wrong with that?
Who should say that my worth is derived from my weight?
It sure is derived from my weight when I'm weighed down with diamonds.
Laugh at my looks but not at my money.
Dollar bills open doors where my nose, my eyes, my height, my weight does not.
Plastic surgery does wonders was the last thing my mother ever said to me.
I stopped speaking to her after that.
I will not shortchange my body to fit in.
I'll shortchange my customers.
That shiny new chrome hood hides a lemon,
and that old junker still runs like a dream.
Who am I to cry when customers whine that the car broke down?
They're the ones with the false noses, false cheeks, false hair, false priorities.

Money was loyal to me when people were not.
Money doesn't care what you look like, what you weigh.
Money will love you like diamonds.
The only double 'D' I ever cared about was the one on the four Cs scale;
it was the only DD that ever cared about me.
Loved ones won't pay for your funeral when you're dead and gone,
but the buildings you erected in your name,
the scholarship funds,
the streets and museum wings
will chant your legacy long after your friends have forgotten you.
Money is ugly, or so they say.
Lucky for me, I'm ugly too.
Good thing my kind—

Penguins
mate for life.

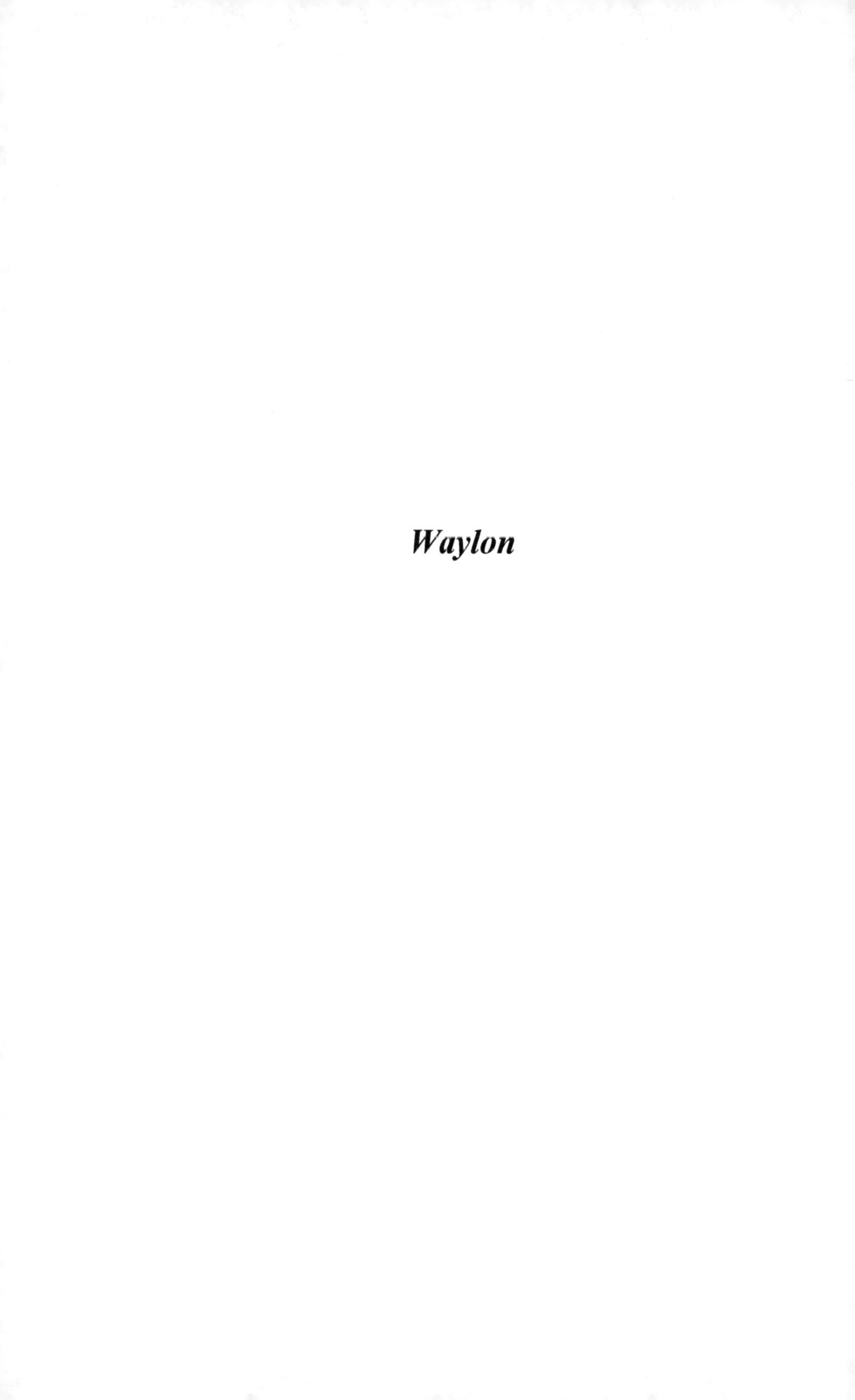

Waylon

Son of Laius

What was I supposed to do when you told me I wouldn't amount to
anything?
How was I supposed to respond to the screams you laid at the doorstep
of my ears?
What did you want me to say when you told me I was a bad apple?
You laid my career path out for me then cast me into the mountains;
You expected me to find my own way.
No shepherd took me in, no Samaritan.
Where could a son of sewers grow?
In the dark, you said.
In the grime, you said.
Go to the places where the stink in the air matched the stink off your
breath.
I did, I did, I did;
I ate what you told me I would eat;
I swam where you told me I would swim;
I did exactly as you told me.
Would I get my gold star then, teach?
Nobody tells me to do anything except fulfill the prophecy.
I'm not bad, baby, I'm fulfilling my role in the ecosystem.
At least I didn't marry my mother—
she died too early for that.
If she had lived—
but what is one woman against society?
What was I supposed to do?
Put in the extra work,
the extra time,
to prove you all wrong?
Why should I have to be the one who rebuilds the walls you tore down
and fixes the foundation you forgot to build?
You did all the work to destroy me and I will not walk barefoot uphill
both ways in the snow.
If you wish for me to be better—
build me better.
Why should I undo what you have done?
Why must I untie the Gordian Knot?
Give me a sword or hack at it yourself.
I wonder if Oedipus gouged out his own eyes,
or if others
placed scales

over them.

Antonia

No One Cared Who I Was Until I Put on the Shorts

Up until the point I put clothes on,
I was myself.
I was also invisible,
And I wanted to be noticed
As we all do.

Put on my costume.
Not latex and leather,
No bomber jacket today, just
cotton and denim.

Now everybody cares.

Gazes all over me like hands,
Lingering leers that hook claws
in my chest
to draw out my fear.

As if you're whispering,
"don't be afraid; fear is for later."
I'm not afraid.
I'm angry.

My existence has become an act of war.
My body is a battleground—
Choose your weapon.

Skimpy shorts and corsets become
Soldiers that get shot and die
in the No Man's Land of the city street.

Long pants and sweaters are now
a retreat
a surrender.

When a man says
"hey sexy"
I want to say
Let's not stand on ceremony, sailor
Your tone of voice is a weapon in which

The words are carved,
"raw her like a piece of meat"
You might as well say it out loud.
Be honest in your villainy.

I am
Spoils to be enjoyed
Blood to be shed
A body to be dumped in the sewers.

And then, an attack from the side:
Kangaroo court calls
"slut or prude?"
Where's the lawyer? No—
Your guilt has been decided
This is a sentencing hearing darling

Slut or Prude?
No matter.
Whichever you choose—
You were asking for it.

I want to strip off my clothes
Hang them where the world can see
Like flags
stand in my nakedness and wonder
if I'm invisible again.

My clothes have become
a symbol of oppression
whether burka or a bikini.

I am an
act of war.
Bare my skin like some people wear masks
I'm a necessary evil
Play the villain take the fall
so the little girls coming up behind me
climb free of the pit
You threw us in before we were even born.

My sin of skin is serious
but not as serious as yours, I fear.

I don my costume and dream
of turning this into real war.
Fire in the streets as every man burns
as I burn inside
when I feel the assault of their eyes
their words slipping into the skin
beneath my clothes.

Nobody cared who I was until I put on
clothes which somehow meant
I chose a side
and got declared guilty.
The jury's all men, you know.

Just like a mask
everybody sees the shorts
nobody sees my face
so I make the mask mine
my body is a bomb and it
declares war.

The Pit

I didn't notice the walls as a child. Just as
we do not notice the light until it is gone.
Not until I saw
the men climbing up
falling
shrieking
dying in pain
for trying to reach the top.

It was so hot.
It was so crowded.
I breathe better now in the mask
than I did in that air
that thick sweat dying despair air.
Air that smells like infection.

Once I saw the walls
I couldn't help
but want to climb them.
All men want to climb them
even those that say they are content
that it could be worse
even those that help the guards kick us
down the wall
they only help so that maybe someday
if they climb
the guards will turn and look away.

At the top where the sun
beat down
beat us down
heated us down
cooked us down
men would stand with ladders.
They sat on the ladders and watched us
talking about their lives
as if we weren't real,
paid actors or animals,
our pain a distant amusing anecdote.

Why didn't you send down the ladders?
Why didn't you raise us up?
The pit is swallowing us
One man gets halfway up and three more are thrown in
You toss us bits of bread and water
and shake each other's hands for it.
Why didn't you bring us into the light?
It bathes you and blinds us
Why didn't you why didn't
    you didn't
          why
            you didn't
doesn't matter anymore.

You're in the pit now.
You're drowning in your vinegar piss,
each stab of pain in your spine
a broken dream.
I will throw down no ladders for you.
Enjoy your imprisonment
and watch us rise.

Burn with Your Cities

They say souls are born burning
and that so many turn to smoldering embers
dormant
water thrown on them until they were drowning

I reignite them all tonight.
You ever seen a true fire, a pure fire?
Forests turned pyres to a goddess we've all forgotten
that's where dragons dwell
right in the heart of the heat.

Seeds sprout and plagues die
in the center of a flame,
Man's first tool and first destruction
unlike our hearts
the fire is true.
Maybe that's where we all should be going.

Burn it all and start over
light our souls all up one last time
one purifying time
one goddess great time
until we scream like dragons
like demons
and Lazarus will rise better
from our ashes
let him see the soft black piles and think
What a bed to lay my head on
What history to tread upon
Maybe our hearts have grown too black like
ashes
in our mouths

Every time we try to fix it
Are we not pruning a rotten tree?
Fire purges plagues
Maybe the only way to save this world
is to kill the worst plague of all.

Your Oppressors

Gotham!
There will come a time when you doubt
the knife in your heart.
Shh shh Gotham
It's all right, we all doubt. Doubt is not what matters
so much as what we do with it.

When you are tempted to stay
           your hand,
stay
           the execution,
remember that if you plunged your hand into their hearts,
you would find nothing to squeeze.

Gotham! Rise! Walk
Upright
In the sun
Let the tall buildings bless you
Finally.
It's all yours now.

Shh shh children
do not let their faces lie;
of course they are afraid!
they know their sinful subtleties
will get them nowhere now.
They deserve that fear.

If we are merciful, what will they learn?
We must be the parents now, Gotham
Gotham
Gotham
Sweet city
You are a wayward child
and I must be your parent.
They cannot get away with this
and a slap on the wrist is not
Enough
with their lies and their greed
They have to know they cannot escape

what comes next
The time for escape is long gone.
No one can get away with their crimes
and we cannot get away with avoiding our duty
The rotten flesh must be cut off
We cannot hesitate now
We must be strong now
Shh shh
It'll all be over soon
For all of us
It'll be over so soon
We won't be coming back from this but *oh*
Neither will they.

Bane Should Have Been a Woman

I want to strip away my clothes and cover my
face
reverse the natural order, and
scream my own rage into the darkness of a cavern that can hide it,
if there is a cavern large enough
to hide such anger.

I am raw and red in places I cannot even see, scrubbed down
and down
and   d
            o
            w
            n
into the very
Heart
of me,
and I want so badly to say:

You think the darkness is your ally.

You think that because you decided you wanted to live a little
dangerous
and be a little
badass
that you understood what darkness was—
that the shadows you chose to enter would

b
        l
                e
                        n
                                d

and
                                d
                        e
                e
        l
b

into

you and make you understand
what it is to be in danger.

You merely adapted to the dark.

I was born in it

m   o   l   d   e   d

by it.

I felt that darkness as it crept up on me from every alley,
in the gaze of every man,
in my own echoing footsteps as I walked
alone.

The darkness lives around me as I am
          twelve,
          thirteen,
          fourteen
years old,
taking the bus by myself and approached by men as old as my father,
told they want to marry me
told I look lovely
told they want my number.
Their words are shadows and they

m   o   l   d

me.

The darkness wraps around me in an elevator
no doors no cameras no witnesses only
darkness
hands made of shadows that touch me and whisper:

          I will only touch you if you want me to
          I will be respectful.

The darkness lives around us
telling us that we are less than you,
that we are only human when you decide we are,
that we are the lesser creatures.

Now you think to enter the darkness and claim it as yours.

You think that you can claim the territory that was
forced
upon us and conquer it
when you have not even earned the right to say you know it.
The shadows do not cling to you.
You walk in the light and it does not
hurt
for it was gifted to you,
soft and inviting.

I didn't see the light until I was already a woman,
and
        by then
it was
                           nothing
                 to me
but blinding.

I was
Born
in the darkness.
I was

m   o   l   d   e   d

by shadows.

I rose up
and I wrapped them around me as a cloak and
I turned myself into a
weapon.

The shadows

b
     e
          t
              r
                  a
                     y   you.

They belong to me.
They belong to my sister.
To my friend,
and my other friend,
and my other friend,
every woman who has walked the path that you laid out for her,

a league of shadows.

You want to prove yourself conqueror.
Go on then.
But we fight—

—to—

—Obliterate.

If we do not kill you, you come back and
          hit
   us
       HARDER.
You

        d   r   a   g

us out
place us underneath the burning light
you cheer,
as if humiliating a woman is what makes you a
man.

You tried to break our bodies but we kept coming.
We are from shadows, and they are

long,

long,

l
   o
      n
        g,

like our memories.

You made sure I was born in the darkness.

I was   m   o   l   d   e   d   by it.

And now, I will use it to

Br
          eak
you.

Death by Exile

Walk.
On a frozen river just outside of town
Surrounds the town
Chokes the town
On the frozen river where bodies lie
underneath and halfway
through

Walk
on the thin, white glass
the slippery ice
the tragic terror mirror
the frozen sea of hands and teeth
For falling in is easier than
climbing back out, clothes so heavy,
each drop of water another piece of debt to
pay with oxygen from your lungs until
it drowns you
freezes you

Walk.
Across
the way you see
men
standing on the other side,
the rich white rule makers born on the other side
raised in wealth and entitlement on the other side
Shouting at you:

Walk:
Faster but not too fast
Careful, step careful
Step smart
Step lightly so as not to disturb
the upside-down ceiling of status quo

Walk
better than the others,
Don't ask why
keep your head down

or the frozen winds of their words
will catch you full in the face and
Blind you
Body parts may fall off from
freezing
but if you still have feet you can

Walk,
even though
the ones around you crashed through,
You can make it.
The tyrants on the other side promise you will.
You have to believe the promises or
You'll start to feel the cold
Hope is a fire in your chest but
the fire melts the ice below
red-black river cracks appear beneath you but you

Walk
       fast
              careful
                      enough
     long
             hard
                     enough
     good
             enough

You can make it if you just

Walk;
ignoring the ache in your stomach
the pain in your bladder
the weight of your eyelids
the cold seeping into your bones
        remolding
your bones into
        ice
the howling of taunting winds
they sound like men laughing
the mirror glass trembling beneath your weight shaking
as you shake
you can't stop shaking

Walk,
say the guards on your side with their
guns at your side the muzzles
pointing at you
the guards laugh at you, where are you going,
stay here, stay on the dirty side of the river
it's safe on this side of the river
the water won't swallow you this side of the river
but the men tell you to come
the gluttonous greedy men

Walk.
this is not death they say

Walk.
this is your chance they say

Walk.
you can reach the other side they say
all you have to do is

Walk,
I say
I have burned your river-noosed city
I have stripped the guards
I have you on my side of the river
my people have the weapons now
we are the guards now
we hold the banks
now
step out onto the ice I say
the gun is at your back I say
but it's okay I say
all you have to do now is

Walk;
like you always told me to do
like you yelled at me to do
like you jeered at me for trying to do
like you punished me for attempting to do
like you promised me if I would only do
I could reach the other side

You carved this river and filled it with debt-doubt-deep-water
You laughed as the cold wind whipped our faces and cut
off our limbs
as we

Walk
starve
bleed
pee
choke
freeze
fight
die
on this
worn-thin rule-bound floor of glass
You starved me on your false hope
well now you get to

Walk
out on the ice
the body-choked blood red
trembling terror mirror
see your reflection
you stand, I say

Walk
rich men fat men bloated men
it is your turn
feel the cold
feel it crack under your weight
feel the death water drag you down
starve on your shred of hope
my army is at your back
and
they
say:
Walk.

Bruce

Postscript

I spoke with Pamela.
She's helping me iron out the holes in my green energy proposal for the board meeting.
She actually looked me in the eye today—
I'm not sure she even realized she was doing it.
The diagnosis only came last month, but once she told me about it, it made perfect sense.
"I could always talk to plants and not people," she said.
"Now I know why."
Sometimes I wonder, if she'd known sooner, what might have changed for her.
Then I look at the paper left for me at workshop station one and read the headline
—another court case, another powerful predator, another woman vilified—
and I don't think anything would have been different at all.
Maybe it would have been worse.
"Pamela's an Aspie" instead of "Pamela's different" and I—
I just don't know.

Got an email from Gordon on my way home.
Easier than a signal in the sky,
but we still have meetings on the roof.
I think he's nostalgic.
He says Eddie left something for me again.
I worry.
At this point I look forward to the day I'll hear on the police radio that he robbed a place,
and it'll be the first I hear about it because he didn't send me a riddle ahead of time.
I tell Gordon to ignore it unless he thinks lives are in danger.
Maybe if he doesn't get the desired response we'll start to have a breakthrough.
Sometimes when the handwriting on the riddle is wavy, I wonder if Eddie is trying to stop himself from writing it.
We'll just add it to the list of things that keep me up at night.

At least Harley's doing better. She's in Europe at the moment.
She's been there since Jack's funeral but I doubt because of grief.
Probably because she knows the statute of limitations on murder.

I was halfway through writing this report when I got an alert from the
kids.
They're making another movie about me.
I don't watch them anymore.
The animated show used to consult me and I appreciate it. They got a
lot of it right.
Plenty of artistic license. Some of the choices made Selina laugh. But I
didn't mind.
The last few, though…
Selina walked out of the theater when we saw the one from 2012.

I don't know how I became a way to uphold the status quo.
Why they put a "b" at the end of my net value instead of an "m."
Why the police are the heroes.
Why being an asshole seems to be what gets them cheers.
Talia was my college girlfriend—
I did an internship with her dad overseas.
Harvey got plastic surgery years ago;
there hasn't been a breakout from the asylum in ten years.
Jason just finished his coast-to-coast motorcycle trip
(because God forbid he go to college
though I suppose I'm lucky I got even one of them to agree to it).
Selina looks more like Eartha Kitt than Julie Newmar.

But I also know there's no stopping them.
They'll tell the stories they want.
At the end of the day all I can do is keep talking to Pamela,
to Harley,
to Eddie,
send Talia more apology flowers
and try to do more, to do better, tomorrow.

Acknowledgements

I do not generally consider myself to be a poet. Originally there was just one poem, *Bane Should Have Been a Woman*. It was written in a fit of rage and trauma, and then it sat in my Notes app on my phone for years.

But slowly, I kept returning to the concept of poems written from a particular point of view. I would find myself furious, depressed, despairing, murderous, and I would write another poem. One day I woke up and I had a collection of them.

It still took a long time before I felt they were in a place to be shared. That they are here for you in print at all is thanks to the support, critiques, encouragement, and feedback of a few individuals:

G, who designed a cover that made my jaw drop, and who sits with me when the hamster is on the wheel;

K, who read the first draft of the first poem and told me it was worth sharing with others;

S, the first person who told me it wasn't my fault;

C, who understood Basil before I did—I swear we'll get that body swap machine working someday;

L, G, and M from writer's group who gave suggestions that took everything to the next level;

And extra deep gratitude to A, who snipped at the rough edges, administered critique with a kind hand, and whipped this collection into shape.

Thank you all. You will be spared when I take over the city.

About the Author

Lincoln Christie is an author, dragon enthusiast, and eldritch being currently lurking somewhere in the United States. You can usually find them on tumblr or haunting the local ramen joint. Their favorite movie is *The Man from U.N.C.L.E.* and their favorite author's name is Agatha.

To find Lincoln's other works, such as their poetry collection and adult science fiction and fantasy novels, you can visit their website lincolnchristie.com. You can also find them at lincolnchristie.tumblr.com where you can watch their embarrassing addiction to sharing memes about their characters in real time. To read their books in chapter-by-chapter updates, get extra content, and see pictures of their cats, you can sign up for their Patreon at patreon.com/LincolnChristie.